GYM RATS:

TOE JAM

To Giselle—

May you have
many happy ice
baths!

Coach Mary

GYM RATS:

TOE JAM

MARY REISS

Janet Venné, Illustrator
Rhonda Paschal, Editor

IrisBlu
publishing

Tucson, Arizona
IrisBluPublishing.com

© 2011 Mary Reiss. Printed and Bound in the United States of America. All Rights Reserved. No part of this book may be reproduced or transmitted in any form or by any means, electronic or mechanical, including photocopying, recording, or by an information storage and retrieval system, except by a reviewer who may quote brief passages in a review to be printed in a magazine, newspaper, or on the Web, without permission in writing from the publisher. For information, please contact IrisBlu Publishing, www.IrisBluPublishing.com.

This book is a work of fiction. Names, characters, places and incidents are products of the author's imagination or are used fictitiously. Any resemblance to actual events or locales or persons, alive or deceased, is entirely incidental.

First printing 2011

ISBN 978-0-9843406-1-3

LCCN 2011929727

ATTENTION BOOSTER CLUBS: Fundraising opportunities for your booster club are available! For more information, please contact IrisBluPublishing, www.IrisBluPublishing.com.

For Morgan

References to the USA Gymnastics level system are used with the permission of USA Gymnastics, www.usa-gymnastics.org.

A special thanks to Marc and Lola.

Introduction

Welcome to the second book in the *Gym Rats* series! If you'll remember, *Gym Rats: Basic Training* is about best friends Morgan and Madison, and their adventures in the gym. The two girls can be found before practice making up routines in the Gym Club's kids' waiting gym. Because the two of them can't get enough gymnastics, their coach, Deb, gives them nicknames: Madison is "Gym" and Morgan is "Rat." *Basic Training* leaves off with Morgan successfully getting her round-off back handspring by herself. Also, we find out that their friend and pen pal they met at camp, Dakota, will be trying out at their gym!

Toe Jam continues the Gym Rats' story and takes on the same format as *Basic Training*. After Morgan and Madison's story, you will find the "Coach's Corner" and the "Drills to Skills" pages where technique and drills are discussed. I hope that you find these sections useful in the gym. Also, at the very end of the book is the glossary. While reading, you will come across certain words in **bold** print. These words are defined in the glossary. A new addition to this book is a section dedicated to gymnasts who have had skills named after them.

My hope is that you enjoyed *Basic Training* and will like *Toe Jam* just the same – or even more! In order to stay up-to-date on all *Gym Rats* information, as well as receive more gymnastics stories, drills and tips, subscribe to *Gym Rats News*, a monthly newsletter designed specifically for gymnasts! Subscribe by going to www.IrisBluPublishing.com.

Thank you for reading!
Mary Reiss

Chapter 1

HANGING BY MY TOES

I was in the dining room reading Madison's notebook entry between bites of cottage cheese.

Dear Rat (AKA Morgan),

Tomorrow starts the last week of school! WOOT WOOT-No MORE SCHOOL! And I can't WAIT to start going the optional days. I'm so glad Coach Deb invited us to come in extra. Do you know who else gets to come in on the optional days? I hope we get to work out with the level 4s - and what if we worked out with the 5s? That would be awesome!

I can't believe that DAKOTA is coming to the Gym Club in 1 WEEK to try out! If she's anything like us GYM RATS, she's really going to like it here! I hope everyone is nice to her. Did you hear Amber tell Leslie the other day at practice that Tina's back hand-spring is ugly? I think Tina heard her, too. Geez Give her a break. Tina just got it! And she's still in Devos! That wasn't cool. I wish there was something we could do to get back at Amber for saying that.

Okay, I have to cut it short cuz I need to study for my last social studies test tomorrow! CU2morrow!

---Gym (AKA Madison)

"Morgan, get back to your homework! It's 8:30!" my mom hollered from the kitchen. I don't know how Mom knew that I was reading the notebook, but she did. I was supposed to be studying for my last math test before the end of the school year.

"Okay! I was just taking a quick break!" I didn't have time to write back to Gym since I had to start studying for my spelling test. I brought my empty dish to the kitchen. "I'm so tired of school! I can't wait till it's over," I complained.

"Four days left. You can hang by your toes for that long," Mom answered. "Let me know when you're ready for me to go over your spelling words with you."

"All right," I sighed and sauntered back to my math book. We had practice until 7 o'clock on Mondays, so I had just a little time to do all of my homework and finish studying for tomorrow's school day. It was already 8:30, and my eyelids were getting heavy…

"Morgan, wake up," my mom lightly touched my shoulder. "Get ready for bed. I'll quiz you on your spelling words tomorrow while you're eating breakfast."

I rubbed my eyes. "Okay," I said as I climbed the stairs to my bedroom. I could see the light to my older sister Allison's room under her door. She just got home from gym – she just finished competing level 8 and was working 9. No doubt she was doing her homework. "How can she stay up so late?" I wondered. I got ready for bed and before I knew it, the sun was shining through my window.

Chapter 2

NICE TRIP

"Jealous," my mom said.

I swallowed my bite of granola. "J-E-A-L-O-U-S." Allison stared at me while I spelled my words out loud. She made a weird face every time I said a letter. It made me second-guess my spelling prowess.

"Right. Zenith."

"Z-E-N-I-T-H."

"Perfect! You're done. Now go brush your teeth and Dad will take you girls to school." I ran up the steps and when I neared the top, I tripped and stubbed my toe.

"Ouch!" My big toe throbbed. I made a big "thump" as I fell.

"Morgan, are you okay?" my mom called from the bottom of the stairs.

"Yeah. I just stubbed my toe." I sat on the top step and took off my sock. Man, it hurt! It already looked a little red, too.

"Hurry up and get going. Your dad's waiting for you in the car."

"Okay." I tried to put my sock back on, but it hurt. I stood up. Ouch! I walked on my heel to the bathroom to brush my teeth. Before heading back downstairs, I stopped in my room to put on my shoes and grab my backpack. I couldn't put my sock or shoe on because my toe was throbbing too much. Dang it! Rather than my sneakers, I took off my other sock and put on a pair of flip-flops. Hopefully Mom wouldn't care.

"What did you do?" Allison popped her head in my door.

"I tripped over the top step and stubbed my toe."

"Nice going," she said and ran down the stairs.

I followed Allison downstairs and got into the back seat of the car where Dad was waiting for us. "Ready for your last Tuesday of school, girls?"

"You know it!" said Allison.

"Yeah. I wish it were Friday, though," I answered.

"Don't worry. It will fly by. What are you two working on in the gym?"

I beamed and blurted out my answer before Allison could even think about starting a sentence. "We're doing lots of level 4 skills and some level 5 stuff. It's really fun! I'm doing **round-off** two **back handsprings** on floor now all the time. We're even working **kips** on bars! I can't wait to go the extra days that Deb invited me to this summer! Madison and I are gonna have a blast!"

"Well, I'm glad you're having such a good time in the gym," Dad said. "And what about you, Al?"

"Oh, you know. I'm working level 9 skills like full **pirouettes** on bars and **double backs** into the **pit** on floor."

"Sounds good. Well, here we are!" We pulled up to my school. "Bye, Kid, have a good day!" Allison stayed in the car because she went to the middle school down the street.

"Bye, Dad!" I hobbled slowly up to the school door.

"Hey, Morgan, what happened to your foot? Did you fall off the beam?" Jessica asked me on the way to my locker.

"No, nothing like that," I answered quietly. I really didn't want to be having this conversation.

"Well, why are you limping? Did you get hurt tumbling?"

"No."

"Well, what happened then?" she pressed me.

"I was running up the stairs this morning and stubbed my toe," I winced. How lame was I?

"Oh…" Jessica was obviously disappointed that I got hurt doing something that didn't involve being upside down. She would have been much more excited about my injury (and so would I) if I had told her that I hurt my toe when my foot slipped as I was doing a back handspring on the high beam, or something cool like that.

I found myself having to explain my limp all day. People kept asking me what happened. Like Jessica, they all thought I hurt it at the gym, doing something really dangerous. It was such a bummer having to tell them that I stubbed my big toe on the way upstairs to brush my teeth.

After school (now, officially, there were only three days left!), my mom picked me up and we went straight over to the gym. I was eating my apple when we picked up Allison at her school.

Packed in my gym bag was the leo I had picked out of the mug that morning. One of my oldest ones, it was black with lime green peace symbols and pink hearts on it. It was comfortable, I'll give it that, but it was bad luck. I wore it on the day that I was working **squat-ons** on bars and my foot slipped off the bar. Then I tripped over the bar and landed on my nose on the **8-inch mat** underneath. I didn't *get* hurt, but it *did* hurt (and when I stood up my nose went numb) and squat-ons scared me for a while after that. Ever since that day, I deemed the "peace" leo bad luck. But I had to wear whichever leo I picked out of the mug – those were the rules!

"How was your math test, Morgan?" Mom asked.

"I think I did pretty good."

"'Well.' You think you did pretty '*well*,'" said Allison. She was such a know-it-all.

"Yeah. All that studying seemed to work. I knew how to do every problem."

"And spelling?"

"I *know* I did *well* on that!" I said, sticking my tongue out at Allison.

"Good. What do you have left?"

"My science project is due tomorrow and my social studies test is on Thursday," I answered.

"All right, we'll get to work as soon as we get home," Mom said.

After I finished my peanut butter and fig sandwich, I quickly wrote to Madison in the notebook:

Dear Gym,
    THREE DAYS LEFT! I had a couple of tests today and just three days of school left! Hey, do you want to sleep over on Friday? We can celebrate SUMMER! I'll ask my mom if you can. It will be cool- we can watch last year's Olympics and eat popcorn. And we can write down our goals for the summer! Oh! And we need to finish our beam routine!
    OK - I'm at the gym - see you in 30 SECONDS!
        Bye!
          -RAT

"Hey, Mom, can Madison sleep over on Friday?"

"We'll see. I'll talk to her mom after practice."

"Okay. Bye, Mom." I walked on my heel to the gym door. Allison ran into the building in front of me.

Mom stopped the car. "Morgan, what's wrong with your foot? Why are you walking on your heel?"

"I stubbed my toe this morning. It's fine," I answered.

"You be careful." Then she left. I turned and shuffled into the locker room. Madison was already there.

"Hey, Rat! Do you have the notebook?" she asked.

"Yup; right here. But I didn't get a chance to write too much; I had to write in the car on the way here," I said as I took off my flip flops.

"Woah! What's wrong with your toe?" Gym asked.

I looked down at my big toe. It wasn't just red anymore. It was definitely purple – and swollen. "Yikes! It looks worse," I said. "I stubbed it this morning running up the stairs." Gym looked at me like I was nuts.

As soon as I said that, I wanted to scoop up my words and shovel them back into my mouth. Amber and Leslie started laughing at me. I shot them a dirty look.

"Does it hurt?" Gym asked.

"Yeah, kind of, I can't really walk on it."

"Did you hear that, Leslie? Rat tripped over her own feet and hurt herself!" said Amber. The two of them cackled as they walked out to the gym.

"Someone needs to teach them a lesson," whispered Madison as we walked out of the locker room.

Chapter 3

ICE COLD

Deb was writing our warm-up on the white board when Madison and I walked out to the gym:

> ### Warm-up
>
> Run 20 laps clockwise
> Run 20 laps counterclockwise
> 100 jumping jacks
>
> Deb leads stretching

"Get started, girls! We have a lot to do today!" yelled Deb.

Madison and I started running clockwise with the rest of the pre-team. We were also warming up with the level 4, 5 and 6s. Allison and the other **optionals** were at dance upstairs. I tried as hard as I could to run, but because I was unable to push off my big toe, I stayed on my heel. It didn't take long for Deb to catch on.

"Morgan! Come over here," said Deb. I ran on my heel over to Deb in the middle of the floor. "What's wrong with your foot?"

"I stubbed my toe this morning," I answered, showing Deb my purple big toe. The bruise had spread all the way down into my foot.

"Wow! That's purple. Let me take a look." Deb led me through the circle of running gymnasts to a **spotting block** where I sat down. "Can you move it?" she asked.

"Sort of. It's pretty sore, though." I showed her how my toe slowly wiggled up and down with the others.

She then compared my right (hurt) toe to my left (healthy) one. "It's definitely swollen," she said. Taking a closer look, Deb lightly squeezed in different spots up and down my toe and foot.

"Oww!" I jerked my foot back.

"Sorry," said Deb. "It feels warm and it's bruised, but it's not broken. You've sprained it. Let me see you stand."

I slid off the block and stood up. "Put your hand on the block and stand on your right foot," said Deb. I did. It really didn't hurt too badly… at first. Then I felt a sharp pain.

"Okay, it hurts," I said.

"Sit down. On a scale of one to ten, how much does it hurt?"

"Ten," I answered.

Deb rolled her eyes. "Okay, let's say that ten is equal to the worst pain you could ever imagine. Now how much does it hurt?"

I thought about it for a few seconds. "Seven," I answered.

"That's more like it. Let me see you walk on it. Try to walk normally."

I gingerly stepped forward on my right foot. It didn't hurt too badly until I pushed off to step onto my left foot. "Ouch!" I said. "That's an eight."

"Have you iced this at all?"

"No, I was in school all day," I defended myself. How did she expect me to ice?

Deb gave me her disappointed look. "Well, that's the first thing you're going to do. Stay here." Two minutes later, Deb came back with a bucket full of ice water.

"No!" I protested.

"Yes. You're going to stick your foot in here for twenty minutes. Be sure to keep moving your foot around." She handed me a sweatshirt and smiled. "Stay warm!"

"Why can't I just use an ice pack?" I asked.

"One, because I said so, and two, because an ice pack won't get between all the little bones in your foot to take down the swelling. Let's go."

I dangled my foot above the ice water. Slowly, I lowered my toe down into the bucket. When the water reached the place where my toes connected to my foot, I jumped. "Yikes! That's cold!"

Deb stood over me like a hawk. "Rat, get your foot in that bucket."

I lowered my foot back into the bucket, all the way down to my heel. A chill ran through my body. All of my muscles tightened up. I started to shiver. I wrapped the sweatshirt around me. My teeth chattered.

Morgan icing her foot

"Be sure to move your foot around," Deb said.

"Okay. It's cold," my lips quivered.

"I know. It'll go numb soon, though. I promise."

I looked at the clock. It was 10 minutes after three o'clock. Dread took a hold of me as I thought about doing this for 20 minutes.

Deb went back over to the girls on the floor. They were doing their jumping jacks. I sat on the block wondering just how long it would take for my foot to go numb. Right now it was stinging! This *couldn't* be good for me. I bit the sweatshirt. I decided to watch the clock to see at what point I wouldn't feel the pain anymore. The clock ticked by slowly. A minute passed after what seemed like an hour. I decided to lie back on the block and cover my face with the sweatshirt. I thought about how the "peace" leo had struck again. When I sat up, only two more minutes had passed! This was going to take forever.

On her way back from the drinking fountain, Madison stopped by my ice station. "How's it going, Rat? Is it broken?"

"No, it's just a sprain," I answered. I wondered what that even meant. It sure *hurt* like it was broken!

"How long do you have to ice?"

"Twenty minutes," I mumbled as I circled my foot around in the icy water.

"Can you work out today?"

"I hope so. She didn't say anything about that yet."

"Girls! Spread out. Let's stretch!" Deb yelled.

"Gotta go!" Madison said as she trotted on her two healthy feet back to the floor.

Chapter 4

Another Klutz!

I watched as the clock's second hand ticked its way to 3:30. *Forty-five, forty-six...* My foot didn't really sting anymore and it was pretty much numb. *Fifty-eight, fifty-nine, sixty!* I pulled my foot out of the bucket. Deb saw that I was going to drip all over the floor.

"Morgan, don't move! Amber, throw Morgan a towel, please!" Amber walked over to the tape station and grabbed a towel. She walked as slowly as she could over to where I was sitting with my frozen foot suspended over the bucket. When she finally got there, she threw the towel at me. It hit me in the face.

"Thanks," I muttered.

"Klutz," she said as she laughed and skipped away.

I dried off my cold foot. It felt really weird now that it was out of the water. It felt hot and cold at the same time. It almost felt like it was asleep. Deb came over. "How does it feel?" she asked.

"It used to be numb but now it's tingly."

"Don't walk on it until the tingle goes away. We need it to thaw out first. Just stay here and I'll get some tape."

Tape? I had never been taped before. This was going to be cool!

Deb came back to tape my foot. First she sprayed this really sticky stuff on it then wrapped a spongy wrap around my foot near my toes. "What's that?"

"It's called "**pre-wrap**." It protects your skin from the glue on the tape," Deb answered. It took her about three minutes to tape my foot and crisscross between my toes.

When she finished she said, "Stand up and see how it feels." I stood on both feet. My toe felt better! "Try standing on your right foot." Slowly, I picked up my left foot. As my weight transferred to my right foot, the pain started to come back.

"Okay, that hurts."

"All right," said Deb. "You're on limited workout until your toe feels better."

"Aw man! I can work out, it's not that bad!"

"Morgan, you need to stay off of it for a bit to let it heal. Otherwise, you'll hurt it more and you'll be out even longer."

"Okay," I said looking down at the white tape on my foot. But I couldn't help but think how unfair it was to be out just as summer workouts were beginning. Dang it!

"I need you to warm up a little bit on the trampoline by bouncing very low with most of your weight on your good foot. Be careful as you circle your arms forward and backwards 100 times. Take turns with Becca. She's doing some ankle **rehab** over there. Then I need you to stretch. Hurry up because your group is on bars."

I got to jump on the tramp for warm-up! All right! I trotted on my heel over to the tramp. This was going to be awesome! This had never happened to me before. The older girls warmed up on the tramp sometimes when they got hurt, but no one on *pre-team* had ever done it. The rest of my group was going to be so jealous! Becca (a level 10 and one of my idols in the gym) was doing some balancing exercises for her injured ankle. I couldn't hold in my smile as I waited my turn.

"Hey, Rat. What happened to your foot?" asked Becca as she stepped off the tramp.

"I sprained my toe," I answered. I didn't want to tell her that I sprained it on my way to brush my teeth, but I knew it was coming. How embarrassing.

"How'd you do it?" I cringed as I told her the story. "Don't worry," she said with a laugh. I hurt myself one time walking across the gym. There wasn't even anything on the floor to trip over – except for my feet!"

"Really?" I was so relieved. Becca was a klutz, too! I stepped onto the bouncy yellow trampoline bed.

Chapter 5

OUT OF THE CHALK BOX

After I finished my warm-up, I went to bars with the rest of my group. "How's your toe, Rat?" asked Gym. She dipped her hands into the chalk box and carefully wiped off the excess chalk by rubbing her palms together. We got 50 push-ups if we clapped or blew chalk in the air.

"It's okay. The tape helps, but Deb said I can't do full workouts until it feels better. What if I lose my round-off back handspring?"

"You won't. I'm sure you won't be out for long. Besides, you get to warm up on the tramp!"

"Girls, get on the bars! I don't want to see any of them open. And rather than talking in the chalk box, I want you to do the **conditioning** on the white board in between turns."

10 Kip Pulls
10 Free Hip Pulls
10 Hollow Body Rocks
10 Leg Lifts

For **kip pulls** and **free hip pulls**, we used **bungees**. A kip pull was a drill that mimicked a glide kip. With one end of the bungee looped around the base of the bars, we lay on the floor with our heads closest to the base holding onto the bungee with straight arms overhead. Then we pulled our arms down to our thighs, keeping them straight, just like on a kip.

The free hip pulls were just the opposite; we had our feet near the base of the bar with our arms straight and our hands next to our thighs. We then pulled the bungee up over our heads with straight arms. This was to help us get the hang of opening our shoulders on **underswing dismounts** and later, on **free hips**.

Deb set up four stations. The first was **glide swings**. If we did these correctly, we could move on to **kips**. The next station was a **cast back hip circle** underswing dismount onto the **gush**. This was the level 4 dismount. Next was the **front hip circle** station. If we made this, Deb let us connect a cast squat-on out of it. Front hip circles were hard, though.

On the last station we did **tap swings** on the **single rail** over the **foam block pit**. Now this

Dropping off the bar in a backswing

was fun! After we practiced our tap swing five times, we dropped into the pit on the **backswing**.

Sometimes we had to fluff the pit if the foam blocks got squished down too far. This usually happened after the level 9 and 10s did dismounts and **release moves** into the pit.

I started on the cast back hip circle station. "Morgan, I don't want you landing on your foot, so no dismounts on that station, and no squat-ons on the next one," Deb told me.

"Okay," I said, disappointed.

"Lucky," whispered Katie. She was afraid of squat-ons and wished she had an excuse not to do them.

What a bummer. I loved doing underswing dismounts! At first I wasn't very good at them. But after I got the hang of it and let my toes rise up to the high bar before I opened my shoulders, I got a lot of height on them. I could just fly through the air and then try to stick my landing.

It was really fun when we had stick contests. In the last five minutes of bars, sometimes we lined up behind one bar and we'd do our dismount one after another and try to stick the landing. If we stuck it, we'd get back in line. If we didn't, we had to sit in our bad leg **splits**, a hollow hold, or something else like that. My favorite contest was when we all had to stick our landings in a row. If one of us missed, we all had to start over! That was really fun; we all got excited and cheered for each other!

Because Deb wouldn't allow me to let go of the bar on my dismount, I did a drill where I did a cast back hip circle underswing, and when I opened my shoulders, I aimed my toes at the high bar and landed with my legs on the gush. I wished I could fly through the air instead of just let my swing putter out.

I moved on to the front hip circle station. Front hip circles were hard. I still didn't have mine. In fact, none of us had our front hip circles except for Amber. She had gotten hers about a month ago. She got her star on the **Star Chart** the first day she made it – she made three of them in a row.

I wasn't very close on my front hip circle. I pushed down on the bar in a **front support**, leaned forward and **piked** around the bar. I finished with my arms bent, my chest bounced off the bar and I landed on the floor below. I wasn't even close! "Morgan, be sure to squeeze your butt as you fall forward; don't pike too soon," Deb instructed. I tried it again. This time I thought about squeezing my butt. I finished with my ribs on the bar. It was a little bit closer than the last one, but I was still far from making it.

Chapter 6

START AT THE TOP

"Okay, girls, rotate to beam!" said Deb. I started to follow my teammates to go wash my hands. "Morgan, you're staying on bars today. The level 5s are coming over next and you'll work out with them. I want you to do whatever

Coach Stephanie wants you to do. She will help you if you need it."

I froze. Stay on bars? With the level 5s? Was she kidding? I guess not since she didn't say anything more and walked over to beam to write the pre-team's warm-up.

Stephanie came over from vault. "Hey, Rat, I hear you hurt your foot so you could do more bars! We're going to have a blast over here. I want you to do the level 5 workout, okay?"

The level 5 workout? Me? I wasn't even a level 4! *She* must have been kidding. But she didn't say anything more and turned to write the level 5 workout on the white board.

Level 5

10 glide swings
10 x 3 cast above horizontal
10 glide kip cast above horizontal
10 long hang kip cast above horizontal
10 cast free hip drills
10 x 5 tap swings
10 tap swing flyaways

I bit my fingernails as I looked at the workout. I could do glide swings and I had done three *casts* in a row before. I don't know if I even made the casts to horizontal, though. And I couldn't do one glide kip cast to horizontal, let alone ten! And free hip drills? Woah! I never even tried one of those before. And then there were **flyaways**! I got to do flyaways? Awesome!

"Look all right, Rat?" Stephanie asked as she set the bars.

"Yeah! But how am I going to do all that stuff?" I asked.

"Well, some of the things you can do by yourself, like the kips and free hip drills. I just want you to try them. Not all of the level 5s have everything on the list. They're just learning, too, so I'll be spotting a lot of the skills."

"Okay!" I answered with a smile. I could handle that.

I tried everything on the list. Although I was a bit nervous to try a flyaway on the high pit bar (I had only done flyaways off the low bar with a heavy spot), I did it with Stephanie spotting me. It was more fun than scary! And it didn't even hurt my toe to land in the foam pit!

I tried the glide kips by myself. Of course I had tried them before and had made them with spot. But I had never made one by myself. After I did the glide, I brought my toes to the bar and tried to kip up. I missed and hit my ribs on the bar. Some of the 5s cheered me on as I went, giving me some pointers after I missed it. It was really fun working with them!

After one of my kip attempts, I saw Amber and Leslie whispering to each other over by beam. They pointed at me and laughed. I didn't even care that they were watching my bad kips. I was having a good time. They didn't get to do them all day like me. They were just jealous.

And every kip seemed to get a little bit better as I tried more and more of them.

Before I knew it, bars was over and the level 5s needed to rotate. Deb came over and told me to stay put for one more rotation. This time though, I had to condition. She had an entire sheet of conditioning printed out for me. There was a lot of stuff on it! When I looked up from the long list that I had to complete, the level 10s were getting their **grips** on and the pre-team was warming up on floor.

I must have had a disappointed look on my face thinking about how I was going to miss out on round-off back handsprings because Becca said, "Hey, Rat. Are you bummed to be working out with us?"

"Huh? Oh, no! I was just thinking about something else."

"Morgan, get started on your conditioning," Scott, the level 10 coach, said. I looked down at the list in my hand wondering how I was going to get it all done in one rotation. I started at the top with **leg lifts**.

Between my conditioning assignments I watched the level 10s on bars. They warmed up by doing tap swings, sets of kip **cast handstands** in a row and sets of **giants**. It was amazing that I was only learning some of the basic skills that they were just warming up with!

After their warm-up, the 10s worked on new skills. Becca was working **double layout dismounts** into the foam pit off the **single rail**. She just started working them after the competition **season** ended. She went to **Nationals** a couple of weeks ago and won vault! It was so cool to know a national champion. The Gym Club had a banner made honoring her and put it up in the gym. It was my dream to have a banner hanging up with my name on it.

Becca Thomas

National Vault Champion

Level 10

Liz was working on her **Gienger*** in the pit. I can't believe that I was just learning how to do a flyaway and she was doing one and catching the bar again! It looked scary – she was so high when she let go of the bar, she fell a long way and landed in a poof of foam blocks. It was crazy being so close to these high-level skills!

*For information on Eberhard Gienger, see page 54.

Liz's Gienger

Eberhard Gienger

Eberhard Gienger was born on July 21, 1951 in Künzelsau, Hohenlohe, Baden-Württemberg, Germany. Gienger was a highly decorated gymnast competing for West Germany during the 1970s. Although he was a strong all-around gymnast, he was most noted for his high bar prowess. The Gienger, a flyaway ½ twist release move on the high bar is named after him. Both male and female gymnasts now commonly perform the skill.

A member of West Germany's Olympic team in the 1972 and 1976 Olympic games, Eberhard Gienger became Germany's Sportsman of the Year in 1974 and 1978. After retiring from gymnastics, he was elected to the German Parliament in 2002 and still represents his constituency today. Known for doing amazing high bar exhibitions in a shirt and tie, Gienger was inducted into the International Gymnastics Hall of Fame in 2007. He is married with three sons.

Eberhard Gienger won the following high bar titles:

1973	European Championships
1974	World Championships
1975	European Championships
1977	World Cup
1978	World Cup
1981	European Championships

References: International Gymnastics Hall of Fame.
www.sportsreference.com

Chapter 7

MORE ICE?

When the pre-team was done with their floor workout, Deb came over to me and asked, "Are you finished with your conditioning, Rat?"

"I just have five more **pull-ups**."

"Great! Do those and wash up. The pre-team is conditioning now."

More conditioning? I was so tired already! My arms felt like they were going to fall off.

"Hey, Rat!" Gym said when I came up to join the group. "I can't believe you had to stay on bars all night."

"I know," I said. "My hands are sore!" My hands *were* sore. They were red from all the swinging I did all night long!

"Okay, girls. We're doing **plyometrics** for conditioning tonight. Set up the blocks around the floor. Morgan, I want you to ice your foot instead. I'll get your ice bucket for you. Take off your tape."

More ice? And in the bucket? This was getting ridiculous.

I got the sweatshirt and a towel so Amber wouldn't have to throw one at me later. I sat on the block and started to peel the tape off my foot. It was sticky, but not that hard to get off my foot because of the pre-wrap. It was harder to get the tape off my toe because there wasn't any pre-wrap there. When I finally peeled it all off, my toe was still sticky from the glue.

Deb brought the ice bucket over. "All right, 20 minutes!"

"Again? How many times do I have to do this?"

"Three times a day, everyday, for 20 minutes until it's better."

"How long do you think it will take to get better?" I asked, horrified that I had to freeze my foot three times a day.

"It could be as long as a week," Deb answered.

"A week?" A week of sticking my foot in a freezing bucket of ice water? And what about summer workouts? They started on Saturday! Tomorrow was already Wednesday. I needed my stupid toe to get better!

I watched my teammates jump up and down and over blocks while the clock crawled to the 20-minute mark. My foot went through the same stages as before: freezing cold, stinging and then numb. It was just as uncomfortable this time around, but I *did* know what to expect, so it made it just a *little* bit easier.

I was done icing at about the same time the rest of the pre-team finished with their plyometrics. Then we all sat in the splits.

Plyometrics

Chapter 8

RESPONSIBILITY

My mom was talking to Madison's mom in the waiting room when practice was over. "It looks like Madison's going to come home with us Friday and spend the night, Kiddo."

"Cool," I said with a sigh.

"What's wrong? Are you tired? We need to get you home so you can finish your schoolwork.

I'll take you home and come back and get Al," Mom said.

At that point Deb came in from the gym. "Carol, can I talk to you and Morgan for a minute?" My mom, Deb and I sat down in the waiting room. Through the window to the gym I watched Becca do her **series** on beam – **front aerial**, back handspring, **layout step out**. She was amazing. "As you know, Morgan stubbed her toe this morning. It looks like a pretty bad sprain."

"You told me that you were all right," Mom said, accompanied by her disapproving look, complete with a raised eyebrow.

Before I could utter my defense, Deb continued. "She can't do much on it right now. I taped it and she spent most of her workout on bars. She also iced it in a bucket of ice water. She had fun with that." Deb winked at me.

"Yikes!" Mom said. "How long until it gets better?"

"It may take a week or more. I just want her to stay off of it until it feels better. I don't want her to injure herself more by compensating for the pain. We're coming up on summer, so she'll have time to make up for it," Deb explained.

"Well, okay," Mom said. "What do we have to do at home?"

"Ice water for 20 minutes three times a day. Morgan knows the drill. And no unnecessary aggravation," Deb said.

"What about workout on Saturday?" I asked, eager to get cleared for my first extra workout of the summer.

"We're going to have to play it by ear, Morgan. I don't want you injuring yourself further."

"Is it even worth having her come to practice while it heals?" Mom dared to ask.

I was horrified and looked at Deb, waiting on pins and needles for the answer.

Deb looked at me and said, "Sure it is. I want her to continue to come in. She'll get in some great bar time."

Phew! Thank goodness she said that. I was sure my mom would have gladly taken me out of the gym for the last week of school.

"Okay, we'll get her better!" Mom answered. "Let's go, Honey."

When we were in the car Mom asked, "Why didn't you tell me your toe was so bad, Morgan?"

"I thought you'd make me skip gym. Besides, I figured it was going to get better by the end of the day. I mean, I just stubbed it," I said.

"All right. I want you to do everything Deb said. You're taking responsibility for your toe here, Morgan. You need to get your ice, be sure you ice it enough and stay off of it as much as possible. I know you don't want to be hurt longer than you have to be."

"Okay," I said. I was *not* looking forward to more soaking in ice water. That night while I got my science project together I dunked my foot in the freezing cold water.

Chapter 9

It's Gone!

My toe hurt again at school, so I limped around a little bit. I still wore flip-flops because it was too swollen to put my sock and sneaker on. Afterwards, Mom picked Allison and me up. We dropped Al off at the gym and then went home; I didn't have gym on Wednesdays. I iced twice more while I did all my homework before going to bed that night.

It still hurt on Thursday. The swelling went down a little, but it was still pretty purple. I put on my sneakers and it was easier to walk at school. Even though I wasn't supposed to, I walked on the outside of my foot so it wasn't so obvious that I was limping. After school I went right to the gym. Deb was in the waiting room when Allison and I got there. "Did you ice today, Rat?"

"Yup. This morning," I answered.

"She did. I was there," confirmed Allison.

"What about yesterday?"

"Three times!" I said.

"Good. I want you to ice right now so you don't miss any practice."

"Now?" I asked in disbelief. But Gym and I were supposed to work on our beam routine in the kids' waiting gym before workout started!

"Yes, now. Go fill up your bucket."

I went back to the locker room to get my sweatshirt. Madison walked in the door. "Ready to go make up our beam routine?" she asked.

"I can't," I said. "I have to ice my foot. Do you have the notebook?"

"Aw, man," Madison said. "Here." She went to grab the notebook from her locker. "Where is it?" she asked. "Did I already put it in your locker?"

I opened my locker door. "No, it's not in here. Did you forget it?"

"No! I *know* I had it in my hands when I walked in here. I thought I put it on top of my gym bag."

"Where could it be?" I asked.

"Morgan! Get going!" Deb yelled from the waiting room.

Where's the notebook?

"I have to go. Keep looking for it! It's *got* to be *some*where," I said.

I carried the bucket of ice water out to the gym with both hands. The cold water sloshed against the sides of the bucket and splashed onto my legs. It was freezing! I accidentally made a few splashes on the floor. The bucket was heavy!

"Be sure to wipe up where you spilled, Rat," Deb instructed. "We don't want anyone slipping on the water."

I wiped up the drops of water with my towel then sat on the block in front of the clock and dunked my foot in. Even though it was June, it felt like winter in the dark gym and like my foot was sitting in a hole in a frozen lake! I pulled the sweatshirt over my head.

I was fifteen minutes in and my foot was numb when Madison came walking over with a disappointed look on her face. "You didn't find it?" I asked.

Morgan carrying her ice bucket

"No," she said. "And do you know what I think? I think Amber and Leslie *stole* it!"

"What? How do you know?"

Madison sat down next to me on the block. Her eyes darted around the gym before she whispered, "Well, when I got here, after I went into the locker room, they came in. I know they saw me put the notebook in my locker and of course, they were whispering to each other. I closed my locker and went into the bathroom to change. When I got back, that's when you were there and we figured out it was missing."

"Where are Amber and Leslie now?" I asked. I couldn't believe my ears. I knew Amber and Leslie were mean, but I didn't think they were *criminals*!

"I'm not sure. They're not in the locker room. They might be in the waiting gym," said Madison.

"Go see if they're in there with the notebook!" I said.

Madison left on her mission. I looked up at the clock. My 20 minutes was up! It went way faster than yesterday. Deb came around the corner as I was drying off my foot.

"Finished, Morgan?"

"Yup," I answered.

"I'll tape you up. Then go ahead and warm up on the tramp so you can stretch with your group."

While I did the same tramp warm-up as I did on Tuesday, the pre-team did their warm-up on floor. I took turns with Becca while she did her ankle rehab.

"What happened to your ankle?" I asked her.

"I was doing a **Yurchenko* half** on vault and landed on the side of my foot. I sprained my ankle pretty bad," she answered.

"Ouch," I said, not knowing what else to say.

"Yeah, it hurt pretty bad for awhile, but it's getting better now. Ice and these exercises help."

"How long ago was it?"

"Four months."

"You still have to ice it?" I asked, wondering if I had four months of ice buckets ahead of me.

"Yup. If I don't, it starts to get sore and swell a little. As long as I still ice it, I can do full workouts."

I stepped onto the trampoline and did my bouncing arm circles backwards.

*For information on Natalia Yurchenko, see page 76.

Natalia Yurchenko

Natalia Yurchenko was born on January 26, 1965 in Norilsk, Russia. She was a highly decorated international gymnast competing for the Soviet Union during the 1980s. The Yurchenko, the round-off entry vault, is named after her. Not only is "Yurchenko" the name of *a* vault, but it is also the name of an entire *family* of vaults for both male and female gymnasts. Any vault with a round-off entry is considered to be in the Yurchenko family. As if that weren't enough, Natalia Yurchenko has a second skill named after her: the Yurchenko Loop on beam.

In addition to the above accolades,

Natalia Yurchenko was the first gymnast to perform the layout mount on beam, as well as the first female to execute two release moves successively on bars. She retired from international gymnastics competition in 1986 and immigrated to the United States in 1999. Currently, Yurchenko resides in Pensylvania with her husband and daughter, and coaches at Parkettes.

Natalia Yurchenko won the following all-around titles:

1981	USSR Championships
1982	Moscow News
	USSR Championships
	World Cup
1983	East Bloc Spartakiade
	Moscow News
	University Games
	USSR Championships
	World Championships
1985	RSFSR Championships
	University Games

References: www.art-gym.atw.hu.
www.gymn.ca/gymnasticgreats. www.gymn-forum.net.

Chapter 10

BARS, BARS, BARS!

After stretching with pre-team, I went to bars with the level 10s. While they warmed up with tap swings, kip cast handstands and giants, I did glide swings on the low bar. Scott gave me some pointers on each of my turns.

"Rat, when you jump to the bar, be sure your head is in between your arms and that your shoulders are completely extended and your arms are straight. Your swing will be much smoother."

"Okay," I said. That was a lot to think about!

Next, Scott told me to work front hip circles. He spotted me on one set of bars and I tried it alone on the others.

Pushing down on the bar in a **front support** so my thighs were touching the bar, I squeezed my butt so my body was in a straight line. Scott held me as I fell forward, making sure I kept my body straight. When I was horizontal, he pushed me forward into a pike position under the bar. I easily finished back in a front support. "Good one, Rat!" Scott said. "Now remember how that feels."

I moved to the next bar. I held the front support until I felt like I was at horizontal. Then

I piked forward, but I didn't make it around the bar back to a front support. Liz, who was behind me in line, said, "Flip your wrists on top of the bar, Rat. Then you'll make it!"

I tried it again. I flipped my wrists on top of the bar, but I didn't make it. "Close, but you just flipped them too late," Liz said.

"Okay," I answered. I moved on to the next bar and tried it again. I fell to horizontal, piked around the bar and flipped my wrists. I finished with my shoulders over the bar and pushed my arms straight to a front support. I made it!

"All right, Morgan!" cheered Liz.

"She made it?" asked Scott.

"She sure did!" Liz confirmed.

Scott said, "Let's see it, Rat."

I did a **pullover** on the bar to get into a front support. I fell to horizontal, piked, switched my hands and pushed back into a front support. I did it again!

"Good one, Rat!" cheered Scott.

"Thanks!" I smiled from ear to ear. I just had to make my next one to get my star! Amber wouldn't be the only one anymore…

"All right, girls. Time to rotate," Scott said. "Morgan, you stay here. Deb's on her way over with your group."

Morgan beginning her
front hip circle

Chapter 11

More Bars!

Deb came over and started writing the bar workout on the white board. "Deb, I made my front hip circle!" I said.

"Is that what all the excitement was about over here?" she asked.

"Yup! And I made two in a row – I just have to make one more to get my star! Can I show you?"

"You can show me when it's time to do them during workout. We need to get started."

Madison came over to the chalk box. "Nice front hip circle, Rat," she said.

"Thanks," I smiled. "Did you find the notebook?"

"No, but I *know* Leslie and Amber took it. They *were* in the waiting gym before practice. I snuck up on them and heard them talking about the notebook. Leslie told Amber that she could read it on the way home in their carpool!"

"*Great*. I can't believe they stole it!"

"I know. We really have *got* to get back at them," said Madison. "My last note to you was my idea about how to do it, too. Now they're gonna know our plan."

"What is it?" I asked, wide-eyed.

"Girls, get started!" Deb said.

"Tell ya later!"

We had five stations: front hip circles; glide kips; casts with spot; **single-leg shoot through**, **front mill circle**; and a conditioning station.

When it was my turn on the front hip circle station, I said, "Deb, watch!" I pushed down on the bar in my front support, just like I did before. I fell to horizontal, piked and switched my hands. My chest bounced off the bar and I landed on the mat underneath.

"You piked too soon, Rat," Deb said. I tried it again and did the same thing. Frustrated, I rotated to the next station.

Amber was up behind me on the front hip circle station. She did her front hip with almost straight arms and casted out of it. She made it look so easy. I glared at her. I couldn't believe that she stole our notebook!

I made my way around the stations back to front hip circles. Before I jumped up to the bar, I reminded myself of all the cues that Scott and Liz had given me earlier. *Push down on the bar, fall to horizontal, pike forward, switch my hands.*

I thought I did it exactly like before when I made it. I fell forward to horizontal and I piked around the bar and switched my hands. I still didn't make it. How frustrating!

I moved on to the next station, which was single-leg shoot through, front mill circle. This was just a little bit scary because we had to switch our hands and fall forward with our chest up. I did the shoot through, switched my hands, pushed down on the bar and fell forward. As I swung underneath the bar, I felt a tear and then a sting on my hand. I dropped to my feet under the bar. I looked down at my hand. A piece of skin had peeled back and was starting to bleed. A **rip**! Ouch! I had never ripped before. *Now* how was I supposed to get my front hip circle?

"Deb, I ripped," I said, staring down at my hand. My teammates huddled around me trying to get a peek at my peeled skin.

"Morgan, go wash your hands. The rest of you wash up and go to beam."

I stuck my hand under the water faucet. "Ouch!" It stung! I rinsed off my hands quickly and patted them dry with a paper towel.

Out in the gym, Deb looked at my hand. "I'm going to cut that piece of skin off, Morgan. Otherwise it'll just peel back and your rip will get bigger."

Reluctantly, I put my hand in Deb's. I squeezed my eyes shut as she clipped the skin. It didn't hurt as much as I thought it would. "Put some of this ointment on it and cover it with a Band-Aid." She handed me a small green jar. "You'll have to wrap a piece of tape around it so it doesn't fall off. Once you're done, get your ice bucket and ice while pre-team is on beam. I want you to condition with your team tonight."

While the pre-team did **cartwheels** and **handstands** on beam, I took off my tape and stuck my foot in the ice bucket. This was getting old. I just wanted to work out! What if I lost all my skills? I already had my cartwheel on low beam – at least I used to have it. What if I couldn't do it anymore? And what about round-off back handsprings on floor? What if I couldn't even do *one* anymore, let alone two in a row! Just then, I heard cheers coming from beam.

"Nice job, Katie! Three for three!" I heard Deb say. "Go put your star on the chart." Katie high-fived everyone. She had just made her cartwheel on high beam.

I wished I were Katie. At this rate, I was *never* going to get any more new skills. Yeah, I made my front hip circle on bars, but I only made it twice! And now I ripped my hand. Who knows how long this would take to get better?

That night I conditioned with my team. We did lots of **crunches**, **v-ups** and **arch-ups**, so I didn't have to use my feet much. Then we did handstand holds and **flexibility** with partners.

"What are we gonna do about the notebook?" I asked Gym.

"I have an idea," she answered. "You know how I said I wrote about how to get Leslie and Amber back for all the mean things they've been doing lately? Well, now that they have the notebook, they're expecting it. So now we're going to have to do something else. But we have to wait until Monday when Dakota gets here."

"What are we going to do?"

"We'll talk about it tomorrow at our sleepover," smiled Madison.

"Okay..." I said. I wasn't so sure about what Madison had in store for us.

Chapter 12

LESSONS FROM A MASTER

I should have been more excited about the last day of school, but with everything going wrong at the gym, I just couldn't be. When Deb looked at my foot last night after practice, she said it was starting to look better, but I had to stay off of it until it felt better. I told her that it was still a seven.

After I went home, I iced it. Then I went to bed and dreamed that my toe was better and I was tumbling. When I went to do my round-off back handspring on floor, I landed on my head. I woke up in a panic! Then I couldn't get back to sleep because I was thinking about losing all of my skills.

Today, school was finally out and Madison was coming over after practice to spend the night. I had to get more excited about this! But I was afraid that Deb wouldn't let me come in for the extra workout tomorrow because of my toe. I was beginning to think that my toe would never get better, and even if it did, what if my dream came true?

I was filling my ice bucket when Madison and her mom came in to the gym with her sleeping bag, pillow and overnight bag. "Hey,

Rat! Happy last day of school! I can't wait for tonight!"

"Me, too!" I faked it. I needed to get excited, but another 20 minutes in the ice bucket was all I could think about…

"I brought some paper so we could write out our plan of attack against Leslie and Amber," she whispered.

"Good idea," I answered. "I have to go ice now. I'll see you out there." I carried my bucket out to the block under the clock. I knew Madison wanted to talk more, but I just couldn't stay there and pretend I was excited. Didn't she understand what I was going through? I dunked my foot in the bucket. The cold water put me over the edge and I started to cry.

I was sure I wouldn't be coming in for tomorrow's extra workout. I couldn't believe that after spending the night at my house, we'd have to take Madison over to the gym for practice and

I couldn't go. This was the worst start to summer *ever*!

Then I started to think. Maybe it wasn't so bad being hurt. I wouldn't have to worry about coming back to a bunch of skills that I couldn't do anymore. I was even starting to get afraid that I would be *scared* of my skills again, even if I could still do them — especially round-off back handsprings. I didn't want to have to go through all *that* again. Maybe I could just be hurt forever. Besides, I got to jump on the trampoline to warm up and work out on bars with the older girls. It wasn't so bad...

"Morgan, can I join you?" It was Becca. She carried her surgical tubing and big rubber therapy bands for ankle rehab.

I wiped the tears from my eyes. "Sure," I said.

"What's wrong, Rat? Wasn't today your last day of school? You should be smiling from ear to ear."

"Yeah, it was. I just can't believe my toe isn't better yet. I mean, it's just a *toe*. And it's only a sprain. It shouldn't be this big of deal."

"True, but if you think about it, toes are used for just about everything in gymnastics. And actually, I've heard that sprains can take longer to heal than breaks sometimes."

"Really? That just doesn't seem right," I said. "If it takes so long to heal, what if I lose all my skills? I mean, what about tumbling? And beam? What about cartwheels? What if I never get them back?"

"Don't worry, Rat. You haven't even lost your skills yet and you're worried about not getting them back! I know what you mean, though. It's hard to think that you'll ever be better when you're right in the middle of being hurt.

Believe me. When I hurt my ankle, I couldn't even *walk* on it for a week, let alone think about tumbling or vaulting on it."

"A *week*? Really? Even with tape?"

"Yes, only I was in a **boot** and on crutches. I was doing exactly what you're doing right now all the time. All I was allowed to do was conditioning and stretching until I could walk on it. Scott didn't want me to fall off bars and injure it more."

"Wow," I said. I guess I didn't have it as bad as that.

"Then after that week, I was only allowed to do bars for a week and a half while I was still in the boot. I eased into low beam and some dance on floor, but that was it. I couldn't tumble for three whole weeks – and once I could, all I did was **basic tumbling**! And the Yurchenko that I hurt it on, well, I didn't try that until a month after I sprained it. And all this was at the beginning of season!"

"Were you nervous that you couldn't do your vault anymore?"

"Of course I was. A Yurchenko half isn't quite like riding a bicycle. I wasn't sure if I would ever get *anything* back like it was."

"You look good now," I said.

"Thanks, Rat. But you know what really helped me, especially when I couldn't do anything? Instead of worrying about not being able to do all my stuff, I visualized myself doing my skills. I thought about what it felt like to do each step of every skill and watched and felt myself do it in my head. It's been four months now and I have gotten back all my skills. I'm even stronger than I was before because of all this rehab I'm doing."

I *definitely* had it better than Becca did. I mean, I'm already walking on my toe and doing bars. And it *was* starting to feel better. Deb still hadn't looked at it today. Maybe I *will* be able to come in tomorrow… In the mean time, I decided that it was time to use some mental imagery.

My 20 minutes was up. Deb looked at my toe. "It looks a lot better, Rat. All this ice and rest is paying off. Let me see you stand on it."

I stood up and took my weight off my left foot. It felt kind of tight, but there wasn't a sharp pain in my foot anymore, just a dull one. "What number is it today?" Deb asked.

"It's like a five, I think," I said.

"Great! I'll bet you're back to full workouts on Monday or Tuesday – with tape, of course."

"Next week?" I asked. "Does that mean I have to miss tomorrow's extra practice?" I was afraid of Deb's answer.

"No, I want you to come in tomorrow. I want you to see what these extra practices are all about, even if you can't do everything. That way you can jump right in next week when you're feeling better."

I breathed a sigh of relief. "Thanks, Deb," I smiled.

"All right. Let me tape this up."

Chapter 13

LATE NIGHT
SCHEMING

"Girls, let's warm up!" Stephanie yelled. The girls started running around the gym. They followed Becca down the vault runway, under the bars, up the stairs to the balcony, over and under the beams, and across the floor diagonals. I was still on the tramp warming up, but Deb told me to jump on both feet this time. With the tape, my foot didn't hurt at all!

After we stretched, the pre-team started on floor. "Morgan, I want you to line up, too. We're starting with our floor **complex** so it won't be too stressful on your foot."

All right! I could start doing stuff! I was a little nervous that it would hurt, but I made it through the floor complex without even feeling my toe. Then the group moved on to **leaps** and **jumps**. Deb told me to go off to the side and work **press handstands** and handstand pirouettes. This was so much better than just being on bars. Don't get me wrong; bars was fun. But it was nice to get back to working out with my group, even if I couldn't do everything they were doing. Besides, I would be able to do it all on Monday or Tuesday!

Morgan in a handstand

After our floor workout we went on to vault. We did some **running drills**, and I was able to do about half of them. Then we did some drills for the level 4 vault, a **handstand flat back**. One drill was to kick up to a handstand on the big **gush mat** and fall flat to our backs, just like the second half of the vault. When the pre-team began running and jumping on the board, Deb had me work on **handstand hops** up **panel mats**. These were hard!

Our next rotation was bars. "Deb, what do you want me to do?" I asked. Certainly she didn't want me doing bars with a rip!

"I'm going to tape you up and you're going to do bars," she said. I looked at her with wide eyes. Was she serious? Didn't she know I had a hole in my hand? "It's going to be fine, Rat. You'll see." She taped up my hand.

I was skeptical. But once I started doing bars, my rip didn't hurt too much. The tape on my hand felt weird, though, almost like I couldn't grab the bar that well. I did everything on bars, but I didn't make my front hip circle again. I tried, but the tape just felt too funny.

After conditioning, workout was over. Madison, Allison and I gathered all of Madison's stuff and Mom drove us home. Allison gave us some ideas for our beam routine. While Madison worked on that, I soaked my foot in a bucket of ice water. "We need to do a cartwheel handstand there," I said.

"Good idea!" said Madison.

"What if you do this into it?" Allison showed us a **body wave**.

"Yeah!" I said.

Later that night over popcorn, Gym and I talked about what we were going to do about Amber and Leslie. "What are we going to do with Dakota?" I asked. I had no idea where Madison was going with this.

"We're gonna have Dakota be nice to them and she's going to be our spy. Because they don't know each other, it won't be hard for Dakota to get on their good side. That way, we can find out what they're saying about us and what they're planning to do to us!"

"What *were* we going to do to them at practice?" I asked. I hadn't been able to read the notebook, so I had no clue what Madison's original plan was.

"You know how they bring the leos that they're going to wear for the week to the gym on Mondays and leave them in their lockers so they don't have to remember them everyday? Well, we were going to get their leos wet and stick them in the freezer overnight so when they went to put them on in the morning for Saturday's practice, they'd be frozen!"

"That's a good one!" I laughed. Wow. Madison was good at coming up with practical jokes. I wish I could have come up with something that good. I still wasn't sure how getting them to hang out with Dakota was going to work. I mean, poor Dakota! "So what's the plan?"

"Okay. First, we're going to call Dakota tonight and tell her our plan. Next, we're going to introduce her to Leslie and Amber and she's going to be super nice to them and gain their trust. Then, when everyone seems to be happy, we'll have Dakota invite us all to a sleepover!" Madison started outlining the plan on her piece of paper.

"What? I don't want to have a sleepover with Amber and Leslie!" What was Madison talking about? She was crazy!

"Don't worry. It's not going to happen," Madison said.

"Dakota's going to invite us to a sleepover and then she's not going to have it?" I was so confused.

"Pretty much. What's going to happen is that they'll be waiting for us to play our frozen leo trick on them, which we're not going to do anymore, and in the mean time, we'll use the scoop that Dakota gathers to play an even *better* trick on them! When Dakota asks us all to spend the night, they'll be so afraid that we're going to do something to them that they won't come! It's perfect! And it all starts Monday."

"All right..." I said skeptically, not knowing just how this was going to play out.

"Let's call Dakota!" Madison picked up the phone and dialed the number.

Chapter 14

EXTRA WORKOUT!

It was 8:30 AM Saturday morning and time to go to the gym for our first extra summer workout! During a breakfast of strawberries, granola and yogurt, I iced my foot. Then my mom brought Al, Madison and me to the gym. Deb, Stephanie, Lisa (the level 6/7 coach) and Scott were in the middle of the floor waiting for all of the groups get there. Leslie and Amber were on the floor already. Madison grabbed me and we stood right next to them and smiled. Leslie rolled her eyes at us.

I brought a roll of tape over to Deb so she could tape my foot. She said, "Morgan, I want you to do what you can during warm-up. If you need to, do the one-footed moves on two feet so you don't hurt your toe. I want you to take it easy today before you try to come back to full practice on Monday."

"Girls, listen up," Scott said. "Here's how these summer workouts are going to work. You will not be split up into your level teams. Rather, we are going to split you up in different ways each day. So the group you are with today is not going to be exactly the same as it will be on Monday and so on. Spread out. Let's warm up!"

I liked Scott's warm-ups. He called out things for us to do like **jumping jacks**, hop on one foot, **tuck jumps**, **burpees**, **toe hops** and other stuff. We had to do them for a specific length of time, then we switched. It beat running in circles! I did most of the warm-up on two feet, just to play it safe. I didn't want to sabotage my chances of doing a full workout on Monday!

After warm-up, we all lined up on the white line around the floor. Scott put us in five groups. Of course, the upper-level group didn't change much, but a couple of level 8s, including Allison, got to work out with the 9/10s. I could tell she was excited.

When it came time to put the pre-team in groups, Scott put Amber and Madison in the level 5 group and put Leslie and me with the level 4s. I was bummed not being able to work out with Madison! Deb saw my face and said, "Remember, Rat, groups change. Work hard and we'll see what happens."

"Okay," I said. I was going to show them! I wanted to work out with the level 5s. Monday was going to be the day!

Our group went to vault first, while Madison's went to floor. In my group were some of the level 4s plus most of the pre-team. We worked level 5 skills mostly. So on vault, we did lots of drills for a **front handspring**. Deb was our coach.

I did most of the slower running drills like **knee-up lunges** and **skips**. Then instead of using the board, Deb had us run from about halfway up the runway and use the **mini-tramp** so we could get used to doing the front handspring over the **table** and into the pit. Because we didn't run full-speed and hit the hard board, I got to do this. It was fun!

Out of the corner of my eye, I could see Madison and Amber on floor working drills for round-off back handspring **back tucks**. Man, they were lucky!

After vault, my group went to bars with Stephanie. She taped my rip and I worked on my front hip circles, kips, **long-hang kips**, tap swings and I even did squat-ons! As hard as I tried, I still didn't make my front hip circle again. I was thinking too much about the tape on my hand catching on the bar. My hand kind of hurt a little bit on tap swings and kips. But that didn't stop me. I hardly even slowed down on bars; I just went from station to station doing my assignments. I wanted to make it into the level 5 group!

Beam was fun; Lisa was our coach. We did a lot of handstands and cartwheels. I mostly stayed on low beam because of my toe, but I could definitely still do my cartwheel down there – I stuck ten in a row! Maybe on Monday I could try it on high beam.

On floor, Scott coached us. We started with a complex to warm up. We did **high kicks**, **turns**, leaps and jumps. Then we moved on to tumbling. Scott had us work not only **back tumbling**, which I did on the **tumble track** because of my toe, but **front tumbling**, too. We worked **dive rolls** onto the 8-inch mat and we did drills for **front handsprings** on the tumble track. It was so much fun!

After floor, we all came back together and conditioned and stretched. It turned out to be a great workout, even though I couldn't do everything. Deb came up to me and said, "Good workout, Rat. I think you'll be good to go on Monday. Just be sure to ice your foot today and tomorrow."

"You got it!" I said with a smile.

Chapter 15

CHANGE ON THE HORIZON?

While I was icing my foot for the second time on Sunday afternoon, I watched last year's U.S. National Championships. Allison set it up so we automatically recorded all of the televised gymnastics meets. I just couldn't believe how good those girls were. I mean, they didn't even *wobble* on beam, let alone fall! It was incredible. I couldn't wait to be that good! The phone rang; it was Madison.

"Hey, Rat! What are you doing?"

"Just watching gymnastics and icing my foot. What's up?"

"Dakota just called and she's in town! She's all ready for try-outs tomorrow – and for the big trick on Amber and Leslie!"

"Cool! I'm so glad that she's going to be here. I hope she likes it at the Gym Club and that she joins our team!"

"I know – then we'll be the Three Musketeers – M, M & D."

M, M & D? Really? We were going to split up "M & M" just like that? I wasn't so sure I liked the sound of this.

The M & M logo from the
Gym Rats' notebook

Chapter 16

DAKOTA'S HERE!

In the summer, sometimes we had practice in the mornings. On Monday, we had to be there at 8 AM. (Allison was lucky – she got to sleep in because she didn't have practice until noon.) I iced my foot while I ate oatmeal. When I got to the gym Madison was already there, and so was Dakota. They were talking in the locker room. "And this is my locker," said Gym. "Rat's is right here. There isn't anyone in this one," Madison said, pointing to the locker on the other side of hers. "You should put your stuff in there."

Here we go, I thought. *The three musketeers...*

"Hi, Rat!" said Dakota when she saw me.

"Hi!" I smiled. There was no way I couldn't like Dakota, even if she might be inching in. She was so nice! "Welcome to the Gym Club!"

Just then we heard Deb yelling for us from the gym. She was ready to start practice.

"So you know the drill, right?" Madison asked Dakota.

"Yup. Sweet as sugar," said Dakota.

"Good, because I'm going to introduce you to Leslie and Amber right now."

I don't know why, but I was a little bit nervous about our plan. I felt like it was going to backfire on us somehow. But Madison was so sure that it was going to work that I ignored my gut feeling. I gave Deb a roll of tape so she could wrap up my toe.

"Dakota, I'd like you to meet Amber and Leslie," said Madison, as sweetly as could be.

"Hi!" said Dakota. "I like your leo," she said to Amber.

"Thanks," said Amber. "Yours is cool, too."

Leslie asked, "How'd you do your hair like that?"

"My mom French braided it upside down," she answered.

"Cool!" said Leslie. Leslie was right; Dakota's hair did look pretty cool.

Madison winked at me. The plan seemed to be working.

"All right, girls! You all have met Dakota by now. She's moving here from Wisconsin and will be trying out here at the Gym Club this week. She was on pre-team at her old gym, so she's got close to the same skills as you all. Please welcome her. Now, start running!"

We jogged in a single file line around the white line. I was so happy to be jogging with the rest of the group! My toe felt great! After warm-up, Deb, Stephanie and Lisa split us into three groups. Because the older girls weren't practicing until later in the day, it was just pre-team through level 5. Deb kept all of the pre-team together today, though, so no one moved into the level 4 or 5 groups. But Dakota was here, so it was still cool!

All through workout, Leslie, Amber and Dakota seemed to hit it off. It really didn't look like Dakota was faking it, either. She looked like she was actually having *fun* with them...

During conditioning, Leslie and Amber were doing their pull-ups on the other side of the bar area. We were doing **handstand push-ups** on the floor bar. Madison asked Dakota, "Well, what did you find out?"

"Hmm? Oh, nothing yet. We're still getting to know each other. But you know, they don't seem that bad. They've been really nice to me today."

"Just wait," I said. "They'll change."

"Yeah," said Madison. "It won't take long."

Chapter 17

REHAB

My toe was a little sore after Monday's practice. I iced it when I got home and then went back to the gym with my mom to pick up Allison. Deb saw us and came out to the waiting room.

"Hey, Rat. How does your toe feel after your first full workout back?"

"It's a little sore," I said.

"That's going to happen. Did you ice?"

"Of course!"

"Good. Come here and I'll show you a couple of rehab exercises you can do."

I followed Deb out to the gym. The level 10s were on vault and Becca did her Yurchenko half. It looked perfect!

Deb grabbed a towel and an old coffee can out of the cupboard where the Gym Club kept the tape and therapy bands.

"Sit down here." Deb pointed to a block. She laid the towel flat on the concrete floor. Now, using your toes, scrunch up the towel."

I grabbed the towel with my toes and began crunching it up. It was hard! My toe and the rest of my foot got tired really quickly.

"Wow, this is a lot harder than you'd think!" I said.

"I know," said Deb. "Does it hurt?"

"No, my foot just feels tired," I said.

"Good. Now what you're going to do is pick up these marbles, one by one, and put them back in the can."

I grabbed each marble with my toes. "This is hard, too!"

Deb smiled. "Rehab isn't easy, but it will really help you get better. Let me show you one more. Stand up and walk over to the drinking fountain by inching your toes without picking up your feet."

It was slow going, but I made my way over to the drinking fountain.

"Nice job," said Deb. "I want you to do these exercises everyday before you ice."

"All three times?" I asked.

"At least twice," Deb said.

"Okay, thanks, Deb."

I finished picking up the marbles with my toes and put the can and towel away. Allison was just walking out of the locker room after her workout.

"Let's go home, girls," Mom said.

I went home to ice my foot before tomorrow's workout.

Chapter 18

HARD WORKOUT

Tuesday's workout was hard. The entire team was there again, just like on Saturday. Scott led warm-ups and split us into groups. This time, Dakota, Leslie and Amber were in the level 5 group and Madison and I were in the level 4 group.

It looked like Dakota was pretty far along for pre-team. She had her front hip circle on bars and was really close to getting her kip. On floor she had a front handspring and could do five standing back handsprings in a row. She could even do an **aerial**!

I was okay about being in the level 4 group, but Madison was not happy. "I can't believe all three of them are in that group," she said. "I was in it on Saturday. Why am I stuck in this one today?"

"It's not that bad," I told her. "I've been in this group *both* days!" I was starting to get annoyed with Madison's attitude. She was bringing me down! Even though it would be fun to be in the level 5 group, I was just happy to be cleared for full workouts!

We started on floor. Stephanie was our coach and we began with basic tumbling. She was *really* picky. If we weren't in the correct position on our skills, she made us go back to the end of the line! Madison had to go back a lot because she was paying more attention to the level 5 group than to what she was doing.

Next we went to vault with Lisa. Half our workout was spent doing running drills and the other half was spent doing front handspring drills. We kept moving through the lines so fast that there was no time for Madison to watch what the other group was doing on bars.

When we went to bars, Scott told me that he didn't think I needed him to tape my rip anymore. I was reluctant, but I did bars without it. It didn't hurt that bad! We worked a *ton* of kips, front hip circles, casts and tap swings. In fact, I made my front hip circle again! But I only made it one time so I didn't get my star yet. Who cares, though – at least I did it again!

Scott raised the single rail over the pit so it was just a little bit higher than the low bar. He spotted us on cast handstands and then he pushed us over so we could learn how to turn and fall to our feet into the pit. It was so cool!

After bars we were washing our hands and Madison said, "I still don't get why they're in the level 5 group and I'm in this one. It's just not fair."

"Aren't you having a good time? Bars was awesome!" I answered.

"I guess, but Amber and Leslie get to rotate with Dakota. I mean, we're the ones that got her to try out at the Gym Club. She should be rotating with *us*!"

"It'll just give Dakota more time to execute our plan," I offered.

After bars, we went to beam with Deb. We started with lots of **relevé** holds and walks. Then we worked leaps and jumps. When there was about half a rotation left, we worked handstands, cartwheels and cartwheel handstand dismounts. On low beam, Deb had us do handstand walks down the beam so we could get used to kicking all the way to vertical. We had a contest to see who could take the most steps and I won! I took seven steps.

Chapter 19

WERE WE WRONG?

By the end of the week, Dakota had finished her tryout and I was in the swing of doing full workouts. At Friday's practice, we still hadn't gotten one word about the notebook from Dakota. She seemed to be way too chummy with Amber and Leslie. And it didn't seem like the three-musketeer thing was happening with *us*, it seemed like it was happening with *them*. "Madison, do you think our plan's gonna work?" I asked her between sets of v-ups.

"I think so. Let's hope that Dakota is just warming them up. She'll get some information from them soon."

"I hope so," I said. "I really just want to get the notebook back and write to each other."

We walked into the locker room. Dakota, Leslie and Amber followed us in. Leslie said, "Bye, guys! I'll see you in about an hour!"

"See ya!" said Dakota and Amber.

After Amber left, Madison said to Dakota, "What did Leslie mean by 'see you in an hour'?"

"Oh, she invited Amber and me over to jump on her trampoline this afternoon."

"And you're going?" asked Madison. She couldn't believe her ears.

I just stood back and watched the two of them, like a tennis match.

"Yeah. Of course. They're really nice to me," Dakota said. "Oh, and you're plan's off. They didn't steal your notebook."

"You *asked* them?" demanded Madison.

"No, I didn't come out and ask them. They were telling me about how you two write in a notebook, then they showed me the notebook that they write in. I told them that you two had lost yours. They had no idea. You know, you should try to like them. They're really nice people," said Dakota.

"Thanks for the advice," said Madison. She was starting to get snotty now. "Have fun at your little party."

Dakota said, "See you tomorrow." Then she turned and left.

"Can you believe her?" asked Madison.

"Well, I guess we could be wrong; maybe Leslie and Amber didn't take the notebook after all."

"But I heard them *talking* about it!" Madison insisted.

"You heard them talking about *a* notebook, not necessarily *our* notebook," I said. "Besides, Dakota just said that they have their own notebook; they even showed it to her. Maybe that's what they were talking about."

"I think Dakota's lying."

"Madison... I think you're taking this a little too far."

"I can't believe you're on their side of this!" Madison yelled and stormed out of the locker room.

Chapter 20

UNLIKELY THIEF

I didn't talk to Madison at all after Friday's workout. I was bummed. What good was summer without my best friend? When I got home, I did my rehab and iced my foot. Then I knocked on Allison's door.

"Allison? Can I talk to you for a second?"

"Uh, yeah. Come sit down." I entered Al's room and cleared a spot on the bed to sit down. "What's up?" she asked.

"I was just wondering if you and Erica ever get into fights." Erica was Allison's best friend. She just finished competing level 8, too.

"Sometimes, I guess. But they don't really last too long," she said. "Why? Are you and Gym fighting?"

"Kind of. We..." I started to explain the notebook situation. "Hey, what's that?" I pointed to a spiral notebook sticking out of Allison's gym bag.

"What? That's nothing," Al said.

"It's not nothing – it's our notebook!" I ran over to her gym bag and grabbed it. It *was* our notebook! "What are you doing with it? Did *you* steal it?"

"I didn't *steal* it. I was just borrowing it."

"Why? What could you possibly need it for?" I demanded.

"I'm sorry, Rat. I was trying to figure out what to get you for your birthday, so I thought I'd look in the notebook to see if there were any clues," explained Allison.

"You took it out of Madison's locker, didn't you?"

"Yeah, I did, but…"

"I can't believe you did that!" I yelled. I took the notebook and left her room. I slammed her door shut behind me.

Chapter 21

M & M

I went right to the phone and called Madison.

"Hello?" Madison answered.

"Gym! Guess what! I found the notebook. *Allison* had it the whole time! Dakota wasn't lying!"

"What? Why would Allison take it?"

"She had some lame excuse about wanting to figure out what to get me for my birthday. But never mind that. We've got the notebook back and it's safe and sound!"

"Well, good! I'm so glad!" Gym responded. "Hey, Dakota called me today."

"She did? What did she want?" I asked.

"She said that she's trying out at two more gyms and doesn't know whether or not she's gonna stay at the Gym Club."

"Oh," I said. "I never thought that she might not stay at the Gym Club."

"Yeah, me either," said Madison. "Hey, do you want to come over after practice tomorrow?"

"Sure! I'll have to ask my mom, but I'm sure it'll be fine," I said. "I'll call you back."

I was so happy to get the notebook back. And I knew Madison would get over being angry. She had painted a picture of what she thought it would be like for Dakota to come to our gym and be our teammate. It just didn't happen that way. And it looked like I had nothing to worry about, either. I was so nervous that Dakota was going to take my place as Madison's best friend. But now I know, no one can take my place. We'll always be "M & M." I sat down and wrote an entry in the notebook.

Dear Gym,

Can you believe the week we had? I'm so glad to have the notebook back. I still can't believe that my own sister stole it! That was not cool.

Well, that's crazy news about DaKota. Do you think she's going to decide to stay at the Gym Club? I didn't know she was trying out at 2 other gyms! Do you know which ones they are?

I know you don't like being in the level 4 group, but I have been having a good time. I mean, I've been really getting better on bars! And it's not like we don't get to do harder skills. I'm so close to getting my front hip circle star! I can't wait for gym tomorrow to try it again. I'm going to make 3 in a row!

Okay, I'll see you tomorrow, Gym. I have to go ice my foot. And man, is it good to have the notebook back!

BFF
Rat

COACH'S CORNER

Hello, Coach Scott here. Injuries are common in gymnastics. From the stub of a toe like Morgan's to a badly sprained ankle like Becca's, injuries happen. To minimize the length of time recuperating, as well as to strengthen the injured area, rehabilitation (rehab) is very important. Of course, it is equally important to wait to begin doing rehab until your injury is beginning to feel better, after a couple days or so of ice and rest. The following are some ankle rehab exercises that can really help.

Single Leg Balance on Trampoline – This exercise focuses on strengthening the small muscles in your foot and ankle.

- Stand in the middle of the trampoline.

- Pick up your "good" foot so you're standing only on your injured foot.

- Balance on your injured foot. Begin with 10 seconds, and work your way to a minute.

- For a challenge, see how long you can balance with your eyes closed.

Resistance Exercises with a Bungee – This exercise works the muscles on all sides of your ankle for better stability and strength all around.

- What you'll need: a bungee (therapy band or surgical tubing)

- Loop the band around your foot so it's resting on the ball of your foot.

- Hold the other end of the band tightly in your hands.

- Point your foot, pushing against the band.

- Flex and repeat 12-15 times.

- Tie one end of the band around an immobile object (the leg of a bed, for instance), making a loop.

- Place your foot inside the loop, with the band resting on the outside edge of the top part of your foot (near your toes).

- Use the resistance of the band as you move your foot outward and sideways.

- Bring your foot in and repeat 12-15 times.

- Place your foot inside the loop, with the band resting on the inside edge of the top part of your foot (near your toes).

- Use the resistance of the band as you move your foot inward and sideways.

- Bring your foot out and repeat 12-15 times.

- Place your foot inside the loop, with the band resting on the top of your foot.

- Use the resistance of the band as you flex your foot toward your body.

- Bring your foot down and repeat 12-15 times.

You may have noticed that Becca is still doing rehab on her injured ankle four months after her injury. This is important because after an injury, that part of the body can be more susceptible to getting injured again. Continuing rehab will only help your injured body part get stronger and stronger to help ward off any further injuries.

Now, it is important to follow your gym's specific protocol if and when you get injured. Morgan didn't go to the doctor to get an x-ray, but your coach may want you to do so. Also, your coach may have different rehab exercises for you to do, depending on your injury. And keep in mind, it is always important to ice!

DRILLS TO SKILLS

Here are a couple of drills for a good front hip circle:

Fall to Horizontal and Hold with Spot:

- Hold yourself up in a tight front support position.

- Your coach should be standing either in front of you or alongside you.

- Keeping your body in a tight position, fall forward to horizontal.

- Your coach will hold your body at horizontal for a count of three so you get the feeling of hitting the horizontal position.

- You can also do this drill without spot on a floor bar.

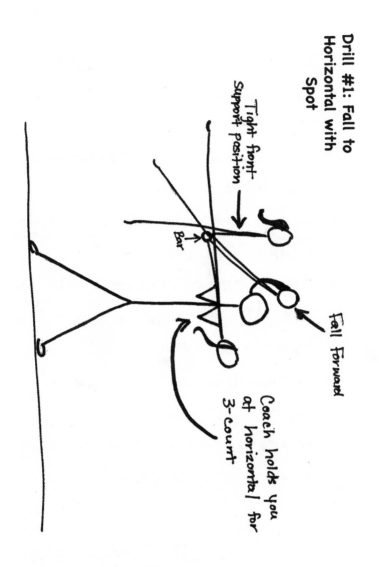

Tight front
Support position

Bar

Fall Forward

Coach holds you
at horizontal for
3-count

Fall Forward to Horizontal with Bungee:

- What you need: a bungee (therapy band or surgical tubing) tied to the base of the low bar so it rests behind your ankles when you are in a front support.

- Hold yourself in a tight front support position.

- With the bungee resting on the backs of your ankles, lean forward to horizontal.

- As you lean forward, lift the backs of your legs up against the resistance of the bungee.

- Be sure to keep a tight body and remain strong against the bungee.

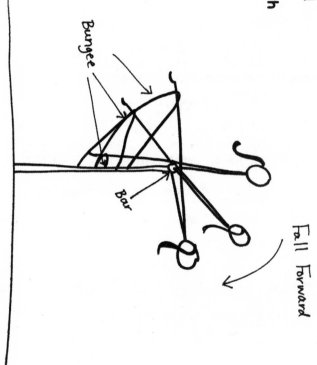

Drill #2: Fall Forward to Horizontal with Bungee

Bungee

Bar

Fall Forward

You can get more information on "Drills to Skills" by going to our Website or by subscribing to *Gym Rats News*, the official newsletter for the Gym Rats! *Gym Rats News* is a monthly newsletter that contains more information about gymnastics, gives you drills and tips on skills, has contests to enter, updates you on the upcoming books in the *Gym Rats* series and lets you share your gymnastics stories!

For more information, just visit www.IrisBluPublishing.com.

GLOSSARY

8-incher: a mat that is eight inches thick

Aerial: a cartwheel without hands

Arch-up: a conditioning move where you lie on your stomach and arch your back so your chest and legs come off the floor

Back Handspring: a tumbling skill where you jump off two feet, arch backward to push off your hands and finish back on your feet

Back Hip Circle: a bar skill where you begin in a front support and circle backwards around the bar back to a front support

Back Tuck: a skill where you perform a backwards salto in the tucked position

Back Tumbling: a series of tumbling skills where you go backwards (usually beginning with a round-off back handspring)

Backswing: part of the tap swing on bars where you swing backwards

Basic Tumbling: fundamental floor skills that concentrate on correct technique and form

Body Wave: a dance move where you fluidly move your body so it makes a wave-like motion

Boot: a device used to immobilize your foot or ankle after an injury

Bungee: surgical tubing or therapy band used for drills or rehab

Burpee: a conditioning series where you begin in a standing position, then squat and put your hands on the floor, kick your feet back to a push-up position, jump your feet back to a squat position and straighten your legs to a standing position

Cartwheel: a tumbling skill where you place each one hand on the floor one at a time while at the same time kicking and straddling your legs over the top like a windmill, finishing on one foot at a time in a standing position

Cast: a skill on bars where you begin in a front support and end up in a hollow body position anywhere from below horizontal to all the way up to vertical (handstand)

Complex: a series of basic skills used together to create a warm-up or workout for an event

Conditioning: a specific workout designed to strengthen specific muscles

Core: the part of your body from your ribcage down to the tops of your thighs

Crunch: an abdominal conditioning move where you do a partial sit-up

Dive Roll: a forward roll that you jump into, getting flight before your hands touch the floor

Double Back: a skill where you perform two backwards saltos in one flip

Double Layout: a skill where you perform two backwards saltos in the laid-out position in one flip

Event: an apparatus in gymnastics

Flexibility: an important part of gymnastics where you stretch your muscles so they become more loose and pliable

Flyaway: a bar dismount where you perform a tap swing and let go of the bar to do a salto to your feet

Foam Block Pit: an in-ground area filed with foam pieces used for training

Free Hip Circle: a back hip circle without touching your hips to the bar

Free Hip Pull: a drill for a free hip circle

Front Aerial: a skill where you perform a front walkover with no hands

Front Handspring: a tumbling skill where you reach forward, put your hands on the floor and flip back up to your feet

Front Hip Circle: a bar skill where you begin in a front support, circle forward around the bar and end up in front support

Front Mill Circle: a bar skill where you split the bar and circle forward around the bar

Front Support: a position on bars or beam where you hold your body up with straight arms so that your thighs are resting on the apparatus

Gienger: a release move on bars where you perform a half-twisting salto usually in the piked or laid-out position and catch the bar

Giant: a circle on the bar where you begin in a handstand and swing in a straight line all the way around the bar back to handstand, keeping your arms straight overhead the entire time

Glide Swing: a bar skill where you swing under the bar (the first part of a glide kip)

Grips: pieces of leather strapped to your hands to protect them and help them grip the bar

Gush Mat: an above-ground pit used for training

Handstand: a position where you stand vertically on your hands

Handstand Flat Back: a vault where after you jump on the board, you do a handstand and fall to your back in a tight body position (the level 4 competitive vault)

Handstand Hops: a drill where you do a handstand and block with your shoulders so your hands hop off the floor

Handstand Pirouette: a skill where you balance on your hands and pick one hand up at a time, turning it before placing it back down again, so you complete a circular motion

Handstand Push-up: a push-up performed in the handstand position

High Kick: a dance skill where you stand on one foot and kick the other leg above horizontal

Hollow Body Position: a position where your body is rounded; the opposite of a tight arch position

Jump: a dance skill where you take off one or two feet and land on two feet

Jumping Jack: a move where you begin standing with your arms at your sides and your feet together, jump and being your feet apart and your arms up, then jump again back to the beginning position

Kip: a bar skill where you do a glide swing, bring your toes to the bar, pull down with your arms and finish in a front support

Kip Pull: a drill for a glide kip

Layout Step Out: a skill where you perform a back handspring step out with no hands

Leap: a dance skill where you take off of one foot and land on one foot

Leg Lift: a conditioning move where you hang straight down from the bar and lift your toes to the bar

Long Hang Kip: a kip on the high bar

Mini Tramp: a small, usually square trampoline used in drills and training

Nationals: the last meet of the level 10 season where the best level 10s in the country qualify to compete

Optionals: the term used for levels 7-elite; those competitors that make up their own routines

Panel Mat: a thin mat segmented so it can stack on top of itself and make a thick mat

Pike: a body position where your legs are straight and together and your hips are bent at a 90-degree angle

Pit: a very thick cushiony mat, usually in-ground

Plyometrics: a conditioning circuit where you continually jump on top of and over blocks for a period of time

Pre-wrap: a spongy wrap used under tape

Press Handstand: a skill where you press your shoulders over your hands and either straddle or pike up into a handstand position

Pull-up: a conditioning move where you hang straight down from the bar and bend your elbows to lift your body and bring your chin over the bar

Pullover: a skill on bars where you begin in a hanging position (or on the floor under the low bar) and lift your hips to the bar and circle backwards around the bar until you finish in a front support

Rehabilitation (rehab): an activity where you strengthen an injured body part

Release Move: a skill on bars where you let go of the bar and then catch it again

Rip: when a piece of skin tears off your hand, usually on bars

Round-off: a skill where you begin like a cartwheel, but you bring your feet together in the middle and land on two feet

Running Drills: drills to enforce the proper running technique, especially for vault and tumbling

Season: the part of the year during which you compete

Series: a connection of dance or acro elements on beam or floor

Single-leg Shoot Through: a bar skill where you cast and place one foot through your hands

Single Rail: a stand-alone bar used for training; can be either a high bar or a low bar

Skip: a skill where you jump off of one foot, bringing your other toe to your knee and switching each step

Splits: a flexibility skill where one leg is in the front of the other and your legs open to a 180-degree angle

Spotting Block: a hard mat used by a coach to stand on in order to better reach a gymnast while spotting

Squat-on: a bar skill where you tuck your knees so both feet land on the low bar between your hands, usually to catch the high bar

Star Chart: a motivational tool used in the *Gym Rats* series where gymnasts place a star next to skills they have accomplished

Table: the vaulting apparatus in gymnastics

Tap Swing: the type of swing that makes up most bar skills (hollow past the low bar, tight arch under the low bar, snap back to a hollow body)

Tight Arch: a body position where you are arched, but still very tight; the opposite of hollow

Toe Hop: a conditioning move where you stand on high toe with your arms straight overhead and you push through your toes so your feet come off the ground (you usually perform many of these in a row, as in a rebound)

Tuck Jump: a jump performed in the tuck position

Tumble Track: a long trampoline used for drills, especially to help in the development of tumbling skills

Turn: a dance skill where you perform a pirouette on one or both feet

Underswing: a bar skill where you lean backwards under the bar and shoot your toes to the ceiling (the level 4 dismount)

V-up: an abdominal conditioning move where you lie flat on the floor with your arms overhead, then fold your body into a pike position and touch your fingers to your toes

Yurchenko Half: a vault skill where you perform a round-off onto the springboard, a back handspring onto the vault table and a salto with a half-twist, before landing on the floor

About the Author

The youngest of eleven children, Mary Reiss grew up on a farm in Corcoran, Minnesota. At the age of five, she began gymnastics. Loving the sport, she continued at North Shore Gymnastics Association in Long Lake, Minnesota until she graduated from high school. Good grades and her level 10 skill set earned her a scholarship to the University of Arizona in Tucson where she competed all four years of her eligibility. Mary then spent the next decade coaching. She continues to enjoy being a choreographer. She is married with one daughter. This is her second book.

Other books by Mary Reiss:

Gym Rats: Basic Training
Book 1 in the *Gym Rats* series!

Read about Morgan as she goes through the highs and lows of going for her round-off back handspring for the first time! Meet her best friend, Madison, and be up close and personal as you read their notes to each other. Also, learn some great drills and techniques for your round-off back handspring from Morgan and Madison's coach, Deb. She even gives you the tricks to learning a high-level skill!

Watch for new titles coming soon!

Mary Reiss also writes a free monthly e-newsletter specifically for gymnasts of all ages! To subscribe, visit our Website at www.IrisBluPublishing.com.

Other projects by IrisBlu Publishing:

Home Fire: Sarah and Charlie by Nancy Ann
Book 1 in the *Home Fire* series!

Publication date: January 28, 2012
For teens and young adults, the *Home Fire* series follows Sarah as she moves to the woods of northern Minnesota. Be a part of her interesting journey as she meets many friends and obstacles along the way.

With All Due Respect

Do you know an older American with a great story? IrisBlu Publishing is collecting the stories of our older Americans to be published in magazine form. These stories should be written by Americans 70 years of age or older and should capture what life was like in the early decades of the 20th Century. Please contact us for more information.

Transplant Stories

IrisBluPublishing is collecting stories, memoirs and personal essays from those people whose lives have been touched by organ donation and transplantation. Please contact us for more information.

Visit www.IrisBluPublishing.com for more information.